Things That Keep Me Up at Night

Marie McKenzie

Marie L. McKenzie, LLC
Orlando, Florida

This book is a work of nonfiction. These accounts are from the author's perspective and memories, and as such, are represented as accurately and faithfully as possible. To maintain the anonymity of the individuals involved, some of the names and details have been changed.

Some names, identifying details, and dates have been changed or omitted to protect the innocent.

Cover designed by: J.L. Woodson:
www.woodsoncreativestudio.com
Interior Designed by: Lissa Woodson
www.woodsoncreativestudio.com
Editor: J.L. Campbell
www.joylcampbell.com.
Editor: Lissa Woodson
www.naleighnakai.com

Beta Readers: MarZé Scott, Solsiré E. Felida, and Terri Johnson

PRINTED IN THE UNITED STATES OF AMERICA

Things That Keep Me Up at Night

Marie McKenzie

♦ DEDICATION ♦

This book is dedicated to the human survival instinct and our ability to overcome. In this memoir, I recount my adversities with profound respect and gratitude for the lessons that each have imparted to me.

♦ ACKNOWLEDGEMENTS ♦

First, glory and honor to my Lord and Savior, for bringing me through. Special thanks to my husband, George, for your love and support throughout this journey, and for showing me what a healthy marriage is. To my family and "village" without whom I may not have survived the journey.

To my mother, Veda Angel, for giving me life and love. I wish you were here to share your story.

Special thanks to Naleighna Kai, without whom this book wouldn't have been written, and for your incredible coaching and editing talents.

To J.L. Campbell my amazing book coach and editor.

J. L. Woodson the cover design rocks.

To NK Tribe Called Success for the incredible support and encouragement. You all inspire me.

To those I did not mention by name and may have forgotten, thank you for all the love and encouragement. May your light never dim and your cup run over into your saucer.

Marie McKenzie

"She stands on the fathoms of memory. Rising above a sea of grief, she curtsies to Sir Death knowing she is no longer ruled by her pain. Survival smiled in return and set fire to the sky."

—Stephanie M. Freeman, Author of *Necessary Evil* and *Nature of the Beast*

ORIGINS

Open secrets are seldom spoken. The way the mind works is curious. Some memories are dear to us and we want to hold onto them forever, while erasing others. However, to share my life journey I must scan my brain for the good and bad. The incidents or memories I want to forget are the ones on perpetual rewind, and some that need to be recalled have been permanently deleted. I often pray that the painful recollections will vanish, like some people, from my life. However, they seem to be glued closer than family.

I grew up in a large extended family in the parish of Clarendon, Jamaica, but wasn't born there. However, life prior to that is a complete blur. My maternal grandparents had lived in England for many years and retired to Jamaica. The five-bedroom house was always filled with people, family, and friends.

On special occasions, we congregated at my grandparents' house, which was the venue for all major happenings.

One such event occurred in the Summer of 1973. One female family member was there for a home birth. The women were excited and busy with the preparations for the baby. While everybody rushed around, I sat on the living room sofa reading a book. I had started reading at an early age and always carried a book in hand.

The man seated beside me was there for the birth, and not directly involved in the process. In those days, men weren't encouraged to take part in the birthing, so he was reading the newspaper, which he spread across my legs and his.

The back of the sofa was against the bedroom wall where the birthing team was occupied. The woman in labor was moaning and groaning in obvious distress. One of the doors leading in and out of that bedroom was to the right of where we sat, and someone could have appeared at any minute.

Since it was their first child, I expected him to show some compassion for her discomfort. He didn't give any indication that he heard his wife, or that he was aware of what was happening so close to where we were situated.

This pervert was bold. I hadn't thought about it then, but it was obviously not his first rodeo. He had to have done this before, with no repercussions.

Without saying a word, he shifted closer as his hand crept up the inside of my legs underneath the paper. I was paralyzed with shock and fear as he attempted to put his fingers in my vagina. The only thing I had the strength to do was clamp my legs shut. However, he kept trying to force his hand between my thighs.

I would not relent and could not stand.

His fumbling seemed to have gone on for hours, although I'm sure it was only a few minutes. When he realized I wasn't moving or opening my thighs, he laughed, pulled away, and continued reading the paper as if nothing out of the ordinary had happened.

I was eleven years old.

Neither of us moved for a while. For the rest of that day and the following weeks the feeling of disgust remained with me. Although I avoided being near him, I don't believe anyone noticed.

Back then, child sexual abuse and domestic violence were rampant in my community. This one man later molested multiple young girls in the family and, from reports, in the district as well. Although the adults knew, nothing was ever done. Open secrets were seldom or not spoken about at all. Would they have acted if I had said anything? I didn't believe anyone would've had the courage to confront him. Not that I thought they were afraid of him, but because my family wasn't known to be confrontational.

Could I have saved some of the later victims if I had told someone about what he did?

The thought still hurts to this day. I never told anyone because I didn't want to make things bad for my family, especially the new mother and her baby. If I spoke up, I believed it would've brought shame and disgrace on the family. Only a few people have heard this story and not in detail. I was in my forties before I finally mentioned it to my aunt, Lyn. I recalled how surprised she had been. However, she didn't confirm what I had learned from another family member, that she too, had been a victim of that same individual. At the time it was mentioned, I was an adult and we were discussing the pedophile in the family and his many known and suspected victims.

To my knowledge, to this day, he has never been confronted. Everyone in the family and majority of the community had knowledge of this.

It's shameful and tragic that the "village" that provided clothing, food and shelter, also would not step forward to protect a child from sexual abuse. Why is that? When I was in my early twenties, I struck up a conversation with a forty-something-year-old woman in the community about the subject. She was unable to think of an answer to my question. However, she relayed a story that shocked me these many years later.

She said, "I know somebody who that happened to."

"Really," I said. "Who?"

"My neighbor, Michelle's six-year-old daughter. Every time she lef for work," she replied in Jamaican Patois, "her boyfriend molest de child."

With eyes and mouth opened wide, I asked, "How do you know that for sure?"

She responded, "They would be alone inside the house for a while, and when she came outside, she can barely walk and always eating a bag of chips."

My tone increased by a few decibels, "Did you tell her mother?"

"No! It's none of my business."

"That is the same damn thing we were just talking about," I yelled. "Nobody gives a rat's ass about the children."

She lowered her head.

"What if it were your daughter?" I continued.

"I would kill him if I found out," she said, now angry.

"How would you find out if everybody shares your opinion?" I scolded.

The conversation ended abruptly and we exchanged goodbyes. The incident was never mentioned again.

By the time I heard the story, the mother and child had relocated and I haven't heard of or seen them since. Over the years, I thought of her and wondered about the woman she has grown into.

In February of 2021, I was a guest on The Stay-At-Home Nurse podcast, where I was interviewed on my role as a Sexual Assault Nurse Examiner. During the episode I spoke publicly, for the first time, about being a victim of childhood sexual abuse.

After I shared the broadcast, family and friends, while offering congratulations on my successes, also expressed shock and sadness about the abuse. Some came forward and shared their experiences with sexual trauma.

One victim was six years old when she was first abused.

As she recounted her experience, she stated that the abuse began with the man's fingers and advanced to penile penetration.

Dear God, I cringe to imagine the torture she endured at the hands of the villain.

As a result of my revelation, I learned, there were more victims and sexual perverts, in my family than I could have ever imagined.

MY MOTHER! MY MOTHER! MY MOTHER!

Sister Veda, as we all called her, was eighteen years old when I was born. I was her second child and didn't share the same father as my brother. She eventually had six children, three boys and three girls, with four separate men. We lived in my maternal grandparents' home with my aunts, uncles, and cousins. I was incredibly young when we relocated to Chapleton, Four Paths in Clarendon. Memories of life prior to that have been overwritten and cannot be recalled. *I have searched all the recesses of my brain without success.*

Many years later, my aunts, Herma and Myrna, married and relocated to their own homes within the same district. We often visited each other and met in church. My mother remained with her children, along with her youngest sister and brother, Lyn and David. The family continued to grow with the addition of their children, among others. Eventually, Lyn also moved out.

As a single mother of six children, she worked hard and did whatever she thought necessary to provide for them. One of the ways she earned an income was to sell produce in the markets in Chapelton, May Pen, or Kingston. On one occasion she left us with the family while she worked in Nassau, Bahamas as a domestic helper. She resumed selling in the markets when she returned home. From the little she had, she gave generously. Sister Veda was kind, compassionate, and would give anyone her last dime and do without.

Her strength and tenacity must be commended and admired. She didn't shy away from hard work and poured all she had into her children. Whatever she had to do to care for us she did without hesitation. Selfcare wasn't in her vocabulary as she would always put others first.

She had many boyfriends: married, single, and occupied. One or two of them were always around. Although they weren't our fathers, I cannot recall them being unkind to, or inappropriate with us children and Sister Veda never sheltered us from her indiscretions.

One night when I was about sixteen or seventeen, we were sitting in her bedroom, chatting as we did on rare occasions. She was in a happy-go-lucky mood. With a wide grin she said, "Laas night mi sidung pan di bed an Zappy pan di chair. Mi sey, Gilbert a knock pon di winda an wa fi cum in." She continued, "mi jus kip quiet an ack like mi nuh de deh." .

My jaw hit the floor when she finished her story of hiding from one boyfriend while she was with another. I couldn't believe she shared that with her teenage daughter and the manner in which it was done. When she saw my shocked and disapproving stare, the laughter stopped and her gaze lowered. The silence was uncomfortable and eventually, I left the room and, we never spoke of that or any similar incidents again.

A few weeks later, the unthinkable happened.

After midnight and I was still awake. I've been short on sleep all my life. My mind is a theater that constantly replays my experiences. Most of what I witness with all my senses, never leaves, pleasant or otherwise. This was a school night, so we had all retired to bed, but as was often the case, sleep eluded me.

I was jarred by bursts of a truck's horn that I recognized as one of the local Johns. The vehicle had stopped at, or near, our gate. Two doors opened and closed. I heard Sister Veda get out of bed in the next room. She must have been expecting someone, or so I thought. Suddenly, a loud female voice called, "Sloopy."

The voice belonged to Miss Susan, my mother's compadre.

"Sloopy, come on," she hollered.

Was that a mating call?

Years later, I became familiar with the popular song, "Hang, on Sloopy" by The McCoys. I then realized that she might have said, "Sloopy, hang on."

Followed by the clanging of the veranda bars being opened, the sound of footsteps entered the living room. The wall was next to the bedroom where my sisters and I slept.

Very soon my ears witnessed what I had assumed only resided in the imaginations of Bee Line authors.

Two women and one man in the room.

The sounds of furniture rocking, mixed with groans, laughter, clanging of bottles and glasses, and bodies slamming into each other blasted throughout the house.

Dear God. There are children nearby.

My younger sisters tossed in bed, which alerted me to the fact that I wasn't the only one awake. Well, even if everyone else had been asleep, they would've been awakened by the sounds of the orgy. My grandparents were asleep in their room, which also adjoined the living room.

The scene played out for hours until early morning.

I didn't sleep that night.

As usual, the incident was never mentioned.

My sisters didn't ask any questions. My mother went on with life as usual, as if she believed the episode was private. Did she actually believe that no one heard?

Get out of my head so I can sleep.

I loved my mother, but was ashamed, and embarrassed about her lifestyle. For many years, even as an adult, I was unable to reconcile her behavior. That affected our relationship, because I could not develop a good mother-daughter bond, as I avoided her company at times.

Sister Veda wasn't a strict disciplinarian when it came to teaching us about relationships with the opposite sex. I recall her advising me not to get pregnant while in school, but not about having sex, how to prevent pregnancy, or not contracting sexually transmitted diseases.

Sister Herma was more direct and vocal on the subject of maintaining virginity until marriage and I appreciated her being in my life because she made a difference.

Parents, be mindful of your speech and actions because your young ones are watching and listening and may decide to emulate you. Think about whether you want to be a positive or negative influence.

To my knowledge, the family never directly addressed Sister Veda's behavior. During high school, I overheard two of my aunts discussing her lifestyle. They listed other single mothers in the community who indulged in similar practices. The women named were friends of my mother, with whom she partied. During the conversation, one of my aunts said, "A money di man dem a pay dem missis."

I gasped in shock at this explanation for my mother's actions.

My little eyes and ears have witnessed things to which no child should be privy.

Sister Veda was the victim of many incidents of domestic violence, oftentimes in our presence. On one occasion, I witnessed one of my siblings' father battering her because he suspected or heard that she had been cheating.

With tears running down her face, she yelled multiple times, "Richard, lef mi nuh. A kill yuh waan kill mi." She pleaded with him to leave her alone and asked if he was going to kill her, while fighting back as best as she could. No one came to her rescue. My grandmother and uncle were sitting on the front verandah, and the fighting was at the back bedroom in the doorway facing the yard outside. Just the way things were at that time. Their disagreement was only between them. Although she was bigger in stature than he was, he clearly had the upper hand. I often wondered what I could have done to help her.

Witnessing incidents like these in childhood often leads to psychological and behavioral issues later in life. I have seen boys who were exposed to domestic violence grow up to be abusers themselves, and girls who have accepted it as a being all right. Domestic violence is not to be tolerated under any circumstances. *It is not ok.*

My mother had health issues and didn't take good care of herself. She was one of those women who poured everything into others, and left themselves last. She had been diagnosed with high blood pressure and took prescribed medication, but, may not have taken them consistently. However, I also knew at that time she smoked cigarettes and consumed alcohol.

In 2001, I received that heart wrenching call.

"Marie, I have bad news," Shirnet said when I answered the phone.

My heart thudded hard and my feet felt heavy as I sat on the nearest seat.

"Sister Veda is in the hospital and they think she had a massive stroke."

My brain was unable to form words to respond.

"Her blood pressure is very high and they cannot get it to go down."

My response, I cannot recall. I lived alone, and the silence and loneliness engulfed me, so I called friends while planning a trip to Jamaica.

I had migrated to the United States years prior. Sister Veda was only able to visit on one occasion and I thank God every day, because during that time, she was able to de-stress and relax, for a change. While she was with me, she often mentioned missing O'Keile, the baby, because it was her first time away from him. He was her last child, a teenager by then, and in high school. When her vacation was over, she was happy to return home, although she could've stayed longer. I encouraged her to extend her time, but she declined. However, she had plans to return to see me.

After the conversation about her hospitalization ended, I knelt by my bed and prayed to God to give us another chance so she could visit again. At that time, my finances and that of my siblings weren't as robust as today. We had been discussing her upcoming trip to Florida and in the process of planning her stay. One of the most important lessons she taught us, was to always save for a rainy day, no matter how small our earnings, and she always had some cash hidden somewhere in the house.

When I arrived in Jamaica a couple of days after she entered the hospital, I knew the end was near. Her breathing was labored and she was lethargic and non-verbal. Although she couldn't speak. When I asked questions, she responded by squeezing my hand, as I had directed her to do. I accepted that there wasn't anything I could do to improve her condition.

While we stood by her bedside, one of the pastors from May Pen saw us and enquired why we were there. Upon being told that the patient was my mother, Pastor Leroy laid his hands on her and prayed. She heard and squeezed my hand.

She died the following day, which was the saddest day of my life. Gone too soon.

The life my mother lived and how hard she worked to care for us have been on replay in my head my whole life. It's upsetting—we hadn't been in a position to elevate her lifestyle and bring her more peace and happiness. I always felt we didn't advance her enough grace for the devoted mother she was. Despite her circumstances, she chose to bring us into the world. Kudos mother.

MY FATHER

He donated a sperm that contributed to my birth and nothing else, so I don't remember much about him. I have one solid memory of him, during which I was terrified. The incident is tattooed in my mind as if it happened yesterday. I was between eight and ten years old at the time and hadn't seen or heard from, or of, him for years.

My family was alerted that he was in the district and his intention was to come and get me. He had informed people that, "I'm here to get Jennifer." In Jamaica we have "pet" names, which we use at home, and Jennifer is mine.

We were still living in Chapelton, Four Paths, and the community rallied around us. Several residents came to our house and stood around to ensure that we were safe. The location and activities of different family members during the ordeal are blurred in my memory. All I know for certain is we were all scared. I imagine that my sister, Ruby, who is two years younger than I and had the same father, was just as frightened. Besides our mother, Ruby is the most generous person I know.

I always wonder why he wanted to take me and not Ruby or both of us. I suspect she was glad she wasn't favored in that case.

Multiple people yelled, "Go call Mass Tye Tye!"

Mr. Williams, affectionately called Mass Tye Tye, was a prominent member of the community and our protector. We felt safe in his presence.

My father's hair was in dreadlocks, he was shirtless, and wore a pair of cut-off jeans. He lifted me in his arms and held me to his chest. All I felt was fear. Most of the details of the ordeal are lost in my mind. We learned he was arrested and released the following day, but I don't know what charges were laid against him. The memory may have been erased because of the traumatic effect his visit had on me. On many occasions, I've tried to picture or come up with even a blur of his face, and failed every time. There is also no recollection of him and my mother together, so it's unclear when he left the family, or if we ever lived together.

No memory good, or no memory bad. My father was almost never around.

Years after I left Jamaica, Ruby reconnected with him and assisted in his care until he died. To this day We don't know if he had any other children.

MY MATERNAL GRANDPARENTS

Mama and Papa – Hezekiah and Emily Angel

My grandparents had nine children, including five boys. My mother was the eldest daughter. They lived in England for many years and opted to have four of my uncles join them there. David, the youngest, was left in Jamaica with the girls. As I was told, to take care of them. Not a good decision. He resented the responsibility, and from my estimation, has never forgiven them.

The family home catered to a large extended family and over time consisted of grandparents, aunts, uncle, grandchildren, cousins, and even non-blood relatives. Can you imagine how chaotic that was sometimes? The one constant moral compass and disciplinarian was my aunt, Sister Herma. She didn't entertain any foolishness from anyone, child or adult. She was also frank in expressing her opinion.

When my grandparents returned to Jamaica, the house, and the living room in particular, was filled with beautiful furniture. My favorite was the cherry wood display cabinet with glass doors filled with colorful, delicate china. My memory pans to seeing my baby cousin sitting on the floor, the doors swinging wide as she gleefully enjoyed the melody of crockery crashing against tile.

"Zan," I yelled as I scooped her up and handed her to my aunt Lyn, who was mortified. We knew Mama would be upset. I cleaned up the mess and could already hear her yelling, "Yuh affi buy bak mi plate dem". Meaning, you have to buy back my dishes.

Life in that home was up and down. Family squabbles among adults and among children, but nothing life threatening ever took place.

My grandparents owned several acres of land and we farmed both plants and animals of various species. You name it, and it was there. Some of my most pleasant memories occurred on the farm. Planting seeds, reaping when it was time, feeding goats and chickens, among others. I didn't like the smell of the pigs and the trough, but I enjoyed their meat. We ate a lot of what we grew—fresh meat, fruits, and other produce. I loved the smell of roasted coffee and chocolate, which came from cocoa beans. We reaped and dried them, then parched and beat them with a mortar and pestle. Oh, the aroma. As children, when we pulled the chocolate out of its shell, we enjoyed sucking on the seeds before putting them away to be dried then parched. I loved those days.

In adulthood, I grew afraid of lizards and was perplexed as to why, because I played with them in childhood. Back then, we made strings from the veins of coconut boughs and used them to form little nooses, which we slid over their necks and pulled them along as our pets. Lizards of all kinds ran up my legs and into my clothing as we worked on the farm. I used to hold them gently in my hands and never hurt them.

I believe my fear started one day when I was sitting on the seat of the outside latrine and my mischievous sister, Ruby, came and threw something in my lap.

"Ruby!" I screamed. My heart pounded as I sprang up from the seat. She giggled as she fled. It turned out to be a lizard. Not knowing what she flung my way terrified me. I'm able to tolerate them now, but no longer embrace them as I did then.

Although we farmed together as a family, when evening arrived, after dinner, the adults and children would separate. Not much socializing outside of general family chores, with the exception of church and prayer meetings. Most times, the adults weren't together; each kept to their own social group, mostly outside the home.

Many evenings we observed as my grandmother dressed and wondered about her destination. Eventually, we discovered that she wasn't always a faithful spouse. It seemed the line of loose women in the family started at the top.

Papa was the sweetest man, kind and gentle. He was quiet and non-confrontational and didn't complain or express anger toward my grandmother. He was a loyal husband until the day he died.

He was a diligent worker and spent a lot of time taking care of his produce and animals. In his later years, he always had a cough. He had seen the doctors a few times for that ailment, but the treatment didn't help. He eventually worsened and died of pneumonia in 1988 at seventy-two years old. It was incredibly sad to see him go. It *is* life—God gives and He takes away.

There was no outward show of affection between the couples in my family. Neither in words nor actions. None for each other or other family members, including children.

Oh, but the whispers. As far as I know, no one confronted mama. In those days, both men and women cheated in almost equal proportion, as I had observed and heard.

People have said my mother followed in my grandmother's footsteps. *Hogwash!* Promiscuity is not genetic. Promiscuity is not a mental disorder, or a biological disease. Each person is responsible for the life they live, the decisions they make, and the consequences.

Could it be that the lack of affection from their spouses drove the women to seek it elsewhere? I'm not saying there weren't any episodes of them being affectionate with one another. It was never visible or voiced. I loved my mother, and I know she loved me and my siblings, despite the absence of expression of it.

Over the years, my family members, especially the younger generation, have changed their attitudes. Today, most are big huggers who generously show love to one another and are not hesitant in uttering, "I love you."

MY SISTER, MARCIA

Marcia was about fifteen-years old when our home was destroyed by fire. Since she was blamed for the lit candle that resulted in the fire, she was banished from the home by my grandmother. As I recall my grandmother shouted, "Mi nuh want har inna mi house."

Some believed that Marcia had been playing with a candle that accidentally ignited the blaze. Since our mother didn't have a place of her own, Marcia went to live with her father, across the street from us.

A few years prior to that, she had started to behave strangely. We didn't understand nor know how to explain what was happening to her. At times she would remove the laces from her shoes, and sometimes cut the shoes in half or leave them off her feet completely, even when the occasion required shoes. She would often leave home and wander all over the community. Sometimes for hours we were unaware of her whereabouts. We were puzzled, unsure of what to do, or how to help her. One day, I had a discussion with my grandmother as to what could've been the cause of her symptoms.

"Is Veda's fault," she replied.

Shocked, I asked, "What did she do?"

Remembering that it was a secret not to be disclosed and that she had said too much, she clamped her lips.

We never broached the subject again, nor did I find out what my mother was supposed to have done.

After she was forced out of our home, Marcia's life rapidly declined. She started smoking marijuana. I learned that she had been the victim of multiple episodes of sexual assaults and rape by men and boys in the community, and beyond. *She too was a victim of the pedophile in the family.* Being on the streets more than at home had exposed her to all sorts of abuse —verbal, physical, and sexual.

Eventually, we discovered she was pregnant. When questioned, Marcia explained that one of the young men in the community had raped her. The family confronted the man she accused and he adamantly denied his involvement. We all believed her. She wouldn't lie. She carried the pregnancy to term, however, the baby was stillborn. Although sad, we were all relieved as she could not have provided a good environment for a child.

Years after I left Jamaica, my mother sought medical answers. Marcia was diagnosed with schizophrenia and hyperthyroidism, among other medical conditions. She often refused to take the prescribed medications and continued using marijuana while she lived on and off the streets. She died in 2005 and although suspicious, her death was never investigated and the circumstances surrounding her passing remain a mystery. We don't believe that she died of natural causes, and the result of the autopsy was questionable.

My only consolation is that my mother was spared the trauma because she had died a few years earlier.

Marcia's life was sad and painful. She was a victim in so many ways. Sadly, we didn't have the resources needed to deal with her mental health and hadn't sought medical treatment for her in a timely manner.

Would earlier diagnosis and treatment have made a difference?

Could we have saved her from the hell she endured? Her journey is one of the reasons I'm committed to using everything God has blessed me with to advocate for victims.

My passion for the homeless, victims of sexual and domestic violence, may have developed due to Marcia's experiences. When she needed help, I wasn't in a position to assist her, but now I'm able to help others. My life as a nurse has opened my eyes and exposed me to victims of all ages, genders, and nationalities. Oh, how I wish I could help them all. *Do what you can, one at a time, Marie.* I must caution myself, whenever I get frustrated at my lack of adequate resources.

One rainy evening, a homeless man came into our Emergency Department. He was wet, and disgruntled. I helped him to undress, and then put on a hospital gown. His feet, sneakers, and socks were dirty and foul-smelling. However, I continued to assist him with cleaning up and provided him with warm blankets in preparations for the doctor's evaluation. While aiding to him, he was grumpy, impatient, and frequently snapped at me. My thought was he must have had bad experiences because I was helping him and yet he was being unkind to me. I chose to not take it personally.

When the doctor was ready to enter his room, I informed her of the odor and handed her my bottle of peppermint essential oil. Anyone who knows me is aware that I have a good relationship with essential oils and I always have a stash handy. This was a special doctor, who would have given him the best care in spite of the stench. She dabbed some of the oil onto her mask and proceeded to the patient's room.

When the treatment plan was completed and it was time for discharge, now in a better mood, he asked me to help him in putting on his shoes and socks. I got him clean socks and dry clothes from the closet we kept in the emergency department for such a time as this. He was also fed with our special turkey sandwich and juice, and given a to-go bag of goodies.

Now, he smiled and said, "Thank you", over and over. When he was completely dressed and ready to depart, I moved toward the door to leave, and for him to follow me out. As I turned to ensure that he had collected his discharge folder and personal belongings, I encountered his lips heading to my left cheek. I stood still.

His lips gently touched my cheek. He was surprised that I hadn't pulled away or expressed anger, and his eyes lit up as his smile widened. He was elated and said, "Thank you."

"You're welcome," I responded. "Be safe out there." He expressed gratitude the way he felt in the moment, and I allowed him.

I didn't scrub my cheek. I don't normally allow my patients to touch me, to be that intimate with me. Later, I thought of Marcia, and wondered if at any time she had experienced kindness on the streets. There are many reasons people end up on the streets. They all have a story. They have families. But God, it could be any of us. Recollections of what she endured, still breaks my heart!

He loudly exclaimed, "Thank you. Thank you," as he continued out of the room, and down the hallway. *Humans haven't treated him kindly in a long time.*

On his way out of the emergency department, he left a children's book for the doctor. During his departure he continued to express his gratitude.

Many years ago, I used to pray that God tormented the people who abused my sister. I wanted them to suffer. My prayer has changed and now I want their lives transformed so that they become helpers of the homeless and other needy individuals.

Use them for Your glory, Lord, I prayed and continue to pray.

MY SISTER, RUBY

Ruby is two years younger and we were remarkably close growing up, that is until she became a teenager and chose the company of her peers. We both drifted towards friends who shared our interests. Like some siblings, our relationship was complicated by disagreements, mostly trivial.

The first time we had a cat-fight, we hurled hurtful words and fists went flying. Our family was shocked because we had a good relationship. However, the malice was usually short-lived and we went back to being besties. She became interested in boys at an early age and enjoyed partying and smoking cigarettes. At the age of twenty-two she gave birth to her first child.

She is a fantastic mother.

There was a time when I wondered if she would travel the road our mother was on. On one occasion, I confronted her about the direction in which she was heading.

She responded, "It *is* in my blood."

'No," I replied, "it *is* your choice."

My life wasn't perfect, but I wanted better for her, because I knew she was capable of more.

Over the years she endured some troubled relationships, which included periods of domestic violence. She survived and is thriving.

The cause of her transformation is unclear, and I've never asked, but it's phenomenal. Now a single mother of two adult children, with one grandchild, she's loving life. Living her best life on her terms and the generational was curse broken at last.

These days when we hear of women in troubled relationships or domestic violence, she often responds, "I don't want anybody to feel sorry for me, my dear. I'm happy without a man."

That always makes me smile. I'm incredibly happy for, and proud, of her.

Ruby had dropped out of school early, but that didn't end her appetite for learning. She would read many books, especially romance novels—give her a Harlequin and she turned the pages all night and day. On one of my visits to Jamaica I went to bed and left her sitting on the sofa reading. In the morning, I woke to see her bright eyed and bushy tailed, lids blinking as she devoured the pages.

"Have you been up all night?" I asked.

She nodded and smiled as she continued reading. She was scheduled for work at ten o'clock that morning.

Ruby returned to school as an adult, trained as a Practical Nurse, and graduated in the top tier of her class. I was so delighted and overjoyed when she showed me her report. Well done, my sister. Well done!

Prior to becoming a Practical Nurse, she was an aide at the Chapelton Hospital, where Sister Herma also worked. Ruby was promoted to Practical Nurse and remained there until she migrated to the United States with her then seventeen-year-old son, in 2015.

My sister is a hard and dedicated worker, like our mother, and her generosity is boundless. On her trips to visit Jamaica, she is known to ship many barrels or boxes with items for friends, family and some residents in the community.

Her progress since arriving in the States has been monumental. When she arrived in 2015, they lived with my husband, George and me for a few months, then leased a house. This wasn't surprising, since she owned her own home and business back in Jamaica. Not being satisfied with renting, she and her son bought a three-bedroom, two-bathroom house in 2018. This was achieved in three short years, without any need for additional help with the down payment.

I've been encouraging her to continue her education by becoming a registered nurse. "Ruby, you should return to school and get your nursing degree," I often said.

"I have to find the time," she responded.

These days we live less than two hours apart, have a great relationship, and are committed to visits as often as life permits. We meet up for shopping and good food. We both enjoy thrifting. I'm obsessed with her cooking, and often put my keto lifestyle on pause when I visit.

AUNT HERMA

The greatest influence in my life has been my aunt Herma, affectionately called Sister Herma. Morally, and in every way, she is my inspiration. When I was in high school, and she was a nurse in Kingston, I spent all my vacations with her. She kept track of when I'd be on school break and came the night before, or the day of, and whisked me off to Kingston to spend the entire holiday period in her home.

During that time, I visited the hospital, where I observed her work and learned a little about the operations of nursing and health care. From as far back as I can recall, I wanted to be a nurse and follow in her footsteps. My dream didn't become a reality until I migrated to the United States of America.

The impact she has had on my life went beyond my career, although I didn't heed all of her counsel. Where morality and discipline were concerned, she was second to none. She was the only one who encouraged the girls in the family to preserve ourselves until marriage, which she proudly accomplished for herself.

Sister Herma lived the Christian life and maintained a close relationship with God, insisted that we attend church services, especially Sunday mornings. Sunday church service and early morning prayer meetings at home were mandatory. Later in life, my sister, Ruby, aunt

Lyn, and I would giggle when recalling how we always fell asleep on the floor during the morning prayers.

Although we strayed from the church, mainly after Sister Herma moved away, most of us have returned. Nothing beats the good foundation laid at home. Like the prodigal son, some of us found our way back home.

Despite the hardships, setbacks, and uncertainties, I'm happy I followed this career path because the greatest joy of my life is caring for my patients, whether in the Emergency Department or in a Rape Crisis Center.

ASSAULTS

The second time I was sexually assaulted I was in high school. The campus of Clarendon College always buzzed with activities. We had several sports teams, so usually a game or two were in session outside of class time. One muggy day, I sauntered down to the sports field. The path led past an unfinished building.

The captain of the football team, whom I knew very well, separated from a group of boys and sprinted towards me. Without uttering a word, he grabbed me by one arm and dragged me into the building. He viciously attempted to rip off my underwear, while he pinned me against a wall.

I played volleyball then, so I was regularly active and physically fit. But I was by no means as strong as he was.

We struggled hard. I was horrified at the thought that he would succeed in raping me and adrenaline kicked in. Both of us were sweating, and I was gasping for breath. He wanted to rip out a part of my soul, and *that* I was unwilling to let go.

He didn't ask for permission as he felt entitled.

I refused to give in and fought as if my life was at stake. The more I resisted, the angrier he got, and the harder he yanked at my clothing. As

I struggled, I lifted one leg to kick at him, and felt his filthy fingers jam into my vagina. The battle intensified.

No words were exchanged. None needed.

Our intentions were clear and polar opposite.

Eventually, I fought him off and jumped through a window at the back. Either luck was on my side that day, or my escape was divine intervention.

To my surprise and dismay, when I exited the building, several male and female students stood around laughing at me. No one attempted to help, although they must have known what happened. Not one word, just laughter. From their expressions, it appeared, some were shocked that I had escaped and so quickly.

Even now, it's hard to believe this happened in daylight, in view of others, and nobody assisted. No one cared. I wasn't the first, nor the last victim on that college grounds. Although I didn't inform anyone in authority, I mentioned the incident to a few teammates and classmates. At the time, the assailant was dating another member of the school's volleyball team. I chose not to tell her about it. Again, I didn't speak up.

I kept my emotions inside and later realized that bottling things up sometimes led to sleepless nights, depression, and other maladaptive behaviors.

Some may say, "But nothing happened. You weren't raped."

My response is *something happened*; I was violated. I was sexually assaulted and that's more than a crime. I didn't give consent, nor was I asked.

From then on, I was more careful of being alone on campus, especially in secluded areas. The incident also made me aware of how socially acceptable that kind of behavior was, even at school. Victims were laughed at and jeered instead of receiving sympathy and support from other students.

At the time of writing this book, I couldn't identify any formal policies and procedures in place to combat sexual violence at that institution. My hope is that there is an organized process in place now.

Multiple female members of my family have been victims of sexual violence. That was the culture we lived in at the time. My family is not unique in this regard. It's disheartening that behavior of this magnitude was allowed and, in some cases, continues.

A young family member was violently raped while walking to school. She was just a little child, less than ten years old. In her case, the perpetrator was apprehended and charged. Back then counseling was non-existent, no intervention for the survivor. From her adult life, I can see, that some of the decisions she made for herself and how she raised her children were probably related to the effects of that trauma. Her mother and I have discussed this, and I suggested she could still benefit from counseling even as an adult. But she didn't want to intervene in her daughter's adult life by suggesting the obvious and encouraging some type of intervention.

Some women decline to speak about their experiences because they're afraid to face the memories, feel ashamed, or have to deal with the responses they may receive. One survivor told me of being raped on the same school grounds years after my departure. She declined to divulge specific details while we spoke. She said, "When I told my classmates, they laughed at me." She added, "I have forgiven them and put it behind me."

I was disappointed and shocked to learn that other students, especially girls, laughed at a victim. I, too, tried to put my assaults behind me. However, they stayed on replay in my head and have kept me up at nights for years. *Memories! Get out of my head, so I can sleep.*

While living in Jamaica, I went through many incidents of being slapped on my butt and groped while sitting or standing in public transport. The buses and vans were usually overcrowded, which inevitably resulted in passengers being in close proximity to each other. Some men and boys took advantage of the situation and fondled females and boys. These incidents were very disturbing.

The most repulsive occurred while I stood in a packed bus, traveling from Four Paths to Chapelton. Passengers were crammed in so tightly, they couldn't stand without leaning against someone else. I suddenly felt uncomfortable because the person directly behind me was standing much closer than normal. Whoever it was, deliberately pressed into me and a firm object was wedged against my buttocks. I turned around, locked eyes with an adult male, and looked down to see him stuffing his penis into his pants, while a creamy, jellylike substance ran down the back of my pants.

That was nauseating.

No one else saw him due to the crowd, and when I scanned the faces of the other passengers who were closest to us, no one appeared to notice.

I was anxious to get off the bus—I felt dirty and needed a scrubbing to get the filth off me. Even more upsetting was the fact that I was wearing my favorite pair of jeans, which hugged me in the right places and thought I may have to burn them. The prospect made me angry because this pair of jeans was gifted to me by my aunt's friend in Kingston during one of my visits.

When the bus stopped in Chapelton, I hightailed it off and scrubbed my pants as best as possible, with toilet paper from my bag while standing at the bus stop. There was no other option, because of errands to run and then hop on another bus, maybe just as packed, to return home.

When I completed my shopping, I rushed home and took the longest shower. No matter how long I bathed, I couldn't feel clean. Of course,

I washed my jeans and kept them because I didn't have the luxury of a flashy wardrobe. My clothes were mostly hand-me-downs. Don't be mistaken, I was grateful for what I had, and loved most of what I wore, but this incident stressed me beyond my means of understanding. I shouldn't have had to consider destroying my favorite clothing due to someone else's careless transgression.

Another disturbing incident occurred on my return to school after a break. I was excited to be back for the new term, my final year at Clarendon College. As I stepped off the school bus, wearing a nice clean uniform and styled afro, I also carried excitement in my heart. This pint-sized, big Afro, brown-skinned-boy I knew from school yelled, "Hey big pum pum gal."

These words were meant to be insulting, implying that I have a big vagina.

I looked at him with furrowed brows and remember thinking, *you wish you knew, right*. After that, I ignored him and continued walking towards school. Some of the boys back then had no respect for girls and a total disregard for basic decency. I don't believe it was because they weren't taught at home. However, I'm certain most were following their peers.

The family of this particular boy was known to me, and his sister was also a student at the school, so I expected a sense of decorum from him. Years later, I got to know him and his family better, and some of his relatives have become my dear friends. I've never recounted the incident to them, or reminded him of it. To this day, every time I see him in person, or on social media, that incident rushes to my mind.

I have been groped and fondled more times than I care to mention, with some incidents so repulsive, they still make me nauseous and tachycardic. Yes, my heart still races at the memory. Yet, I remained silent.

My nursing career spans twenty-three years, and introduced me to the Sexual Assault Nurse Examiner (SANE) position. The training I received opened a new world for me and I dove right in without hesitation, and have never regretted it. Some of the most rewarding times have been when I cared for victims of sexual and domestic violence and homelessness. People affected by these adversities come from all walks of life—all ages, genders, nationality, socioeconomic status, and race.

As a Sexual Assault Nurse Examiner, I understand the dynamics and conflicting emotions of victims and what they go through. The same emotions plagued me. Victims of domestic violence and sex crimes don't always make a report and some remain silent for a lifetime. Some come forward years later to share because they realize they have been hoarding this secret, which is affecting their life negatively and preventing them from moving forward. Holding on to this secret also leads some victims to choose unhealthy lifestyles to cope with the shame and stress.

"I cannot talk about it," one victim told me. " It still makes me so angry."

There are others who expressed anger after discovering that the perpetrator had assaulted other women in their circle who also hadn't reported the crime.

"If they had reported, I wouldn't have been raped." This particular survivor was justifiably angry as she expressed her disdain.

Evil resides in all forms.

I share about female victims, but rest assured, there are also males of all ages, and more than you can imagine. Our boys and men are not exempt from sexual and domestic abuse, although it isn't talked about much. Like the female victims, some are ashamed, scared, and afraid of public humiliation. Although I don't mention female perpetrators, they do exist, but seldom mentioned. In my career as a sexual assault nurse, I've never attended to someone who has been violated by a woman offender.

One male victim in his thirties visited our emergency department because he had been raped. He said, "I'm so ashamed that I *allowed* him to rape me."

He relayed that he was violated by his uncle at nine years old, and here he was, in his thirties being victimized yet again.

"He looked just like my uncle, so when he held my hand and pulled me into the room, I just followed as I did when I was nine years old."

Heartbreaking.

If you have been affected by any kind of abuse, do the memories still keep you up at nights as they do me?

Please, get help, it's never too late.

HIGH SCHOOL

One incident transpired in high school where my reaction was, *Oh my God! I'm involved in this scandal.*

To this day, I can't believe I did that. I'd been dating a football player at the time. The football team had an away match in another parish. The day they were leaving, a few other female students who were dating football players and I hopped on the bus and went with them. Totally out of my character. Something I never thought I would've been a part of. Without any approval from my mother or family, I left home on an adventure. I'm not sure how many days we were gone. The team stayed at a hotel near where the game was being played. We were provided with accommodation and meals, which I assumed were covered by the team managers.

When we returned to school, we were called to the principal's office. The assistant principal informed me that she was disappointed in me. She didn't have to tell me—I was disappointed in myself. I don't recall what my mother said about the incident, or the family's reaction. Our fellow students looked at us differently. Many were shocked that we went and that I was involved because I was an industrious student and had never been in trouble. Some used to refer to me as "stush." That meant they considered me prideful. My modus operandi was to do what was expected of me, get good grades, and not find myself in trouble. But I didn't always stay out of it.

During my mid-teen years, I agreed to go on a casual date with an acquaintance who was older than me. He was an adult and my mother would not have approved, so I didn't ask for permission or tell anyone. This was one of the times my impulsive side dominated. At the end of the evening, he drove to a hotel near May Pen and booked a room. He had told me he was meeting someone, which turned out to be a lie. When we got to the room and I refused to have sex with him, he stormed out and left me stranded miles away from home without money. I had no way of communicating with my family, since cell phones weren't available then and we didn't have a house phone. Now, it was dark and I had no transportation home.

I walked into the lobby and the lovely young man at the desk realized something was wrong. "You look upset," he said. " What can I do for you?"

With my head lowered, I explained what had happened.

He reassured me that he would keep me safe. He told me, "Since the room is paid for, I will change the room number and you can stay here until morning."

He had tried but was unable to obtain transportation to take me home. "Thank you so much," I gratefully replied.

Oh, how relieved, I felt. He had restored my faith that there were good men in the world. I returned home the following morning to a frantic family and tons of questions. The perpetrator was someone my mother knew, so she confronted him. At the time of the incident, he was unaware of who my mother was, and I was unaware that he knew my mother. She was so angry that he had attempted to violate her underage daughter, and she relayed that he had apologized.

I wasn't blameless in the situation because I agreed to date an adult. However, my agreement to go out with him, didn't translate to consent for sex. Furthermore, sex with a minor, even if he or she consents has always been illegal. Some adults are cursed with perverted minds and don't care about age limits.

Parents, protect your sons and daughters by maintaining an open line of communication about sex education and life in general. Let them feel comfortable speaking with you on any topic.

THE VILLAGE

For a long time I used a smile to hide my inner turmoil. While growing up, although not destitute, my family was poor.

During high school, I visited my friends' homes, but hesitated to invite them to mine. Theirs were always clean and beautiful, even if they weren't lavish. Food and drinks were never in short supply. At my house, meals were limited and sometimes other basic necessities were lacking. However, with the help of the community we did the best with what we had and survived.

Many "helpers" contributed to my journey. From my community, through schools and the different neighbors and friends encountered in the places I have resided. They are too many to list and I don't want to leave out anyone. From those who provided encouraging words, friendship, prayers and financial support, to name a few of my gifts. Many of the boys and girls I met and played with in kindergarten, primary, and high schools are now men and women who have remained dear to my heart. Some of the adults who contributed to my success are still alive and remain in my circle.

One of the most profound acts of generosity was the impact of the "village" during the summer of 1980, while I was a lower sixth form (U.S. first year community college) student at Clarendon College. The family home was totally destroyed in an accidental fire and we lost almost everything.

Despite the adversities, my time at Clarendon college, from 1974 to 1980, were some of the best years of my life.

When I recall the multi-paged letters my schoolmates and I used to share during school breaks, it makes me smile. Letters that I kept for years, but lost during the house fire. These days we don't write letters. We text, email, send Facebook and WhatsApp messages, and on rare occasions, we Zoom or FaceTime. Given so, the pandemic has made the last two contact methods more popular. Oh, how technology has changed and given us more means of keeping in touch and at a more rapid pace. It warms my heart to connect with people from my past and read their stories on social media.

Without the "village" I wouldn't be where I'm today because I may not have survived my childhood.

A significant part of our upbringing was church attendance, which was mandatory on Sundays, and hats for women were considered the norm.

One member of our community, Miss Lou, owned a department store in our district. Miss Lou invited me to her store, on multiple occasions, to select whichever hat I loved. I remember a beautiful blue half hat with lace that I wore to church and conventions on many occasions. Today, a hat like that is known as a "fascinator' and is quite expensive.

At times I felt embarrassed that we didn't enjoy a life of plenty as others around us, however I'm grateful that we had enough because of the assistance we received. I have evolved from comparing myself to others, by learning to love, and appreciate myself for who I am.

To the community of Chapelton Four Paths, Clarendon, and the numerous people who have helped me and my family throughout the years, thank you.

We will forever be grateful.

THE NEITAS

I met the Neitas family when I moved next door to them in May Pen, Jamaica. They're among the most generous and sweetest people in the world. Boyd and Hya Neita are like angels walking among humans. Open hearted, warm, and a breath of fresh air. They've been like parents to me since shortly after we met.

Over the years, whenever they went out of town, I would house and dog sit. One time, I prepared the dog food, cornmeal with chicken, and placed it in the kitchen sink to cool. Usually, I turned on the faucet and plugged the drain to catch water in the sink to help with the cooling process. I had planned to go back to my home and return later to feed the dogs when the food cooled.

A few hours later, I headed towards their house. When I arrived at the gate, a stream cascaded down the driveway into the street. *Oh my goodness!* My heart pounded as I flung the gates open and ran into the driveway. I fumbled with the key to open the door. Beads of sweat moistened my skin as I went inside.

Dear God, the house was flooded. I was horrified. In the kitchen, I discovered I had left the faucet open. I turned it off and stood there with water under my feet. All I could see was water, water, and more water. *Help, Lord! What am I going to do?*

Some of the floors were carpeted which made matters worse. When

I was able to move, I dried up as best I could. What was I going to tell them? I anxiously awaited for them to come home. They came back later and when I told them what happened, Boyd said, "Don't worry about it. Accidents happen."

Relief flooded through me, although, knowing them, I hadn't expected anger. The incident reinforced how amazing they were. They were so gracious and understanding, even though they had to rip out and change all the carpets. Incredibly, they trusted me to house and dog sit the next time they went out of town. I never left the faucet running again.

I looked forward to visiting them at nights. Boyd always had a bucket of oranges or mangoes, which the three of us would peel and eat, mostly Boyd and me. It always made me feel special that he waited for me to share with him. He was one of the few men I grew to trust due to the negative experiences encountered with the opposite sex.

I enjoyed our friendship. Even when they relocated to Guinea, Africa, we kept in touch. Their three children, Donna, Wayne, and Denise, became my siblings as we bonded over time.

When I moved to the United States, we were again neighbors in Tamarac, Florida. This wasn't planned, but the Lord works in mysterious ways. We didn't live next door to each other this time, and our relationship remained as close as it had ever been.

The Neitas were always there for me during the hills and valleys of my life. They attended my graduations and cheered me on in my successes. When my mother died, they offered sympathy, words of comfort, and financial assistance. Boyd and Hya were also instrumental in brokering a peaceful settlement when my first marriage ended.

Boyd Neita is as timely a person as anyone I know. The man is incredible. He walked me down the aisle for both of my marriages. My first wedding in Jamaica in 1986 was scheduled for 9:00. At exactly that time, we were walking hand in hand down the aisle. When I remarried in 2002, we were in Lauderdale Lakes, Florida, with walking time again scheduled for 9:00. However, we were asked to delay because most of the guests hadn't arrived. Who would have thought that a wedding in Jamaica would be timelier than one in the United States?

Today, we are firm, supportive friends, and I'm forever grateful.

I learned many valuable lessons from Boyd and Hya that have also helped me to become the woman I'm today. They taught me to be more loving to friends and family, and to value time by being punctual. They shared with me the importance of integrity, to keep my word, and be kind to myself and others. Boyd made me realize there are men of value and integrity in the world. Whether family, friend or acquaintance, members of the opposite sex are able to foster long term platonic relationships.

Boyd and Hya, I appreciate you and will always be grateful for your friendship and generosity.

THE BRISCOES

The Briscoes have been part of my life for more than thirty years. I first met the eldest of five sisters, Faithlyn, when I worked at the Jamaica Public Service Company, in May Pen. She, a fresh-faced new high school graduate, and I, a secretary.

The memory still brings a smile. At the time, my duties included testing job applicants. However, we weren't testing on that particular day. When I informed her of such, she looked at me and said, "Why can't I do it today?"

I understood her frustration with having to return on another day. You see, she had to travel many miles, and on public transport. In addition, the fare was extremely high. I relented, and she flew through the testing with excellent scores.

Faithlyn was hired as a clerk. She was a model employee with an aptitude for learning, and rose rapidly through the ranks of the company. While working in May Pen, we bonded quickly and became close friends, often visiting each other's homes. One of my secretarial skills was typing, and very soon I had a student. Faithlyn had an appetite for acquiring new skills, even those not required for her position. Her willingness to learn, and assist wherever needed, made her loved and respected by all.

As our friendship grew, I met other members of her family, including her parents and four sisters. I came to know Shirnet, sister number four, an effervescent teenager, while she was a student at Vere Technical High School in Clarendon. Shirnet, immediately stole my heart and, to this day, I'm struck by her magnetic personality. She was like my little daughter-friend and we have a special relationship.

A few years after Faithlyn arrived at the office in May Pen, a position opened in the Mandeville office, and she was transferred there. Within a noticeably short time, she was the leader of the branch. Faithlyn, from the beginning, displayed the leadership characteristics required to advance to the top of her field. I recall the excitement we all shared when she was recommended and selected from a list of candidates.

Rose, another of the Briscoe sisters, was employed at the May Pen office, after Faithlyn. She also became my roommate. Her work ethic was similar to Faithlyn's and the staff and managers loved her.

When the time came for me to migrate to the United States, the staff held a send-off in my honor. Pictures of Shirnet and Rose singing at the function are in my album. I can still hear the melody of their harmonious voices, although not the words. It was a joyous occasion.

During my early visits to Jamaica, the family and mine competed to decide at which house I would spend most of my time. My family always lost. However, the battle was usually between Faithlyn and Shirnet.

One particular visit, we decided that I would stay at Shirnet's and visit Faithlyn for a couple of days. However, the day after I arrived at Faithlyn's home, a car drove up, but we weren't expecting visitors. When we investigated, we discovered that it was Shirnet.

"What are you doing here?" we asked.

"I'm here for Marie," she replied.

I kept my lips sealed and left the fight to them. In the end, I left with Shirnet. She always won. She was lovingly strong-willed, and no one had the courage to argue with her. *Not out of fear, but because we all adored her.* Since then, every time I visit Jamaica, there is no question as to where my base will be. The Briscoes are my family on all levels. Whenever any of them visit Florida, my home is their home and vice versa.

One time Faithlyn visited with her husband, Sean, their new baby, and her dad. It was after my divorce and I lived in a one-bedroom apartment. When friends and family visit, we don't discuss hotel reservations, we make do with what we have. We all stayed in the apartment, and the visit was memorable.

The family is strong in the Christian faith and doesn't miss an opportunity to attend church. So, when Sunday arrived, we all went to church. Her father didn't pack anything specific for church, so he was without an appropriate shirt. Not a problem though, my long-sleeved, white shirt saved the day. That's the nature of my relationship with the whole family, and we assisted each other in many ways.

Shirnet, in particular, came to my aid whenever I needed any monetary transactions done in Jamaica. She was my go-to for communication and sending money to my mother and other family members, whether I had money to repay her or not. When my mother was rushed to the hospital, my relatives needed to pay for the brain scan prior to it being scheduled. By the time the information reached me, the payment had already been made by Faithlyn and Shirnet. Before I arrived in Jamaica, I had received updates from the sisters. They had visited my mother.

There's a saying— "Good friends are better than pocket money."

They, Shirnet mostly, transported me wherever I had to go. She was with me the first time I went to see my mother, and the following day when I went to the hospital and received the devastating news of her death.

We were on our way to the ward and ran into her treating physician.

"Did you hear?" The doctor asked.

"Hear what?" We asked in unison.

"Your mother died early this morning."

"Why weren't we notified?" I questioned.

"We tried to call, but was unable to reach anyone with the phone number listed," she replied.

We thanked her and walked away. Shirnet, hugged me and said, "I'm so sorry, Marie."

I could only shake my head in response as the tears rolled down my cheeks.

My sister, Ruby, arrived as we prepared to leave, and we gave her the sad news. We needed to make arrangements and other family members had to be informed. The hospital staff advised me of the outstanding bill, and of course I acknowledged it. I expected to have a balance to pay and thought there would be time given to settle. Even a few hours, or a day. However, on our way out, we were informed that the bill had to be paid prior to my leaving the hospital. That was shocking because it was unreasonable to expect people to be walking around with thousands of dollars. I was told by the staff that was the policy in Jamaica. Again, Shirnet came to the rescue, and the hospital bill was finalized then. At that time, I wasn't amused, but often laugh when recalling that escapade.

When I met and decided to marry George, the Briscoes were a huge part of our celebration, although the wedding took place in Florida. Shirnet, my maid of honor, Faithlyn, one of the Bridesmaids and, Rose—who was pregnant—all took the trip to celebrate with us. Oh, how I wish Mom and Dad Briscoe could have accompanied them. I also wished my own mother had lived to attend.

Although my wedding planner had given guests information for local hotels, that was unnecessary. This trip, I lived in a two-bedroom townhouse, which provided more comfortable accommodations. We thoroughly enjoyed the occasion. George also became a member of the family by the end of their visit, even though it was their first meeting.

Shirnet, the practical joker, often spoke to George in Patois. We all laughed, as he looked to me and others for interpretation, which we often ignored.

"Jaage, ow yuh duh?" she said with a wide grin as we all laughed. Meaning, "George, how are you?" She later sent him an English-Patois book so he could brush up on his Patois before visiting Jamaica.

Today that fresh-faced, high school graduate I met so many years ago is Doctor Faithlyn Wilson, wife, mother of two adult sons, and Principal at El Instituto de Mandeville Preparatory School in Mandeville, Jamaica. The other four sisters are all successful, with spouses and children of their own.

Our many trials and triumphs cemented our relationships and the Briscoes have a home in my heart.

Thank you Lord for bringing them into my life and introducing me to yet another set of trustworthy men.

MY CAREER PATH

My first job after high school was with Doctor Anderson, our community physician, who had a private practice. From him, I learned the importance of attentive listening and diligence to details. We developed a great working relationship. Aside from greeting the patients, I was also his official scribe. One of my duties was to write out prescriptions. I meticulously wrote the name of the patient, the drug, and directions for use on small envelopes.

It's fitting my first work experience was in the healthcare field, as my desire had always been to become a nurse like my aunt Herma. Later, I detoured into other areas of work, but eventually returned to the medical area.

My first introduction to patient care was as a Home Health Aide, where I cared for the elderly in their homes. This ignited my passion for nursing and led to further training as a Certified Nursing Assistant and then Licensed Practical Nurse, prior to achieving the level of Registered Nurse.

In 1998 I joined the Emergency Department (ED) staff at the Memorial Regional Hospital in Hollywood, Florida, after earning an Associate's Degree in Nursing from Broward College. Prior to that I worked as a Licensed Practical Nurse (LPN) in Nursing Homes and a

Short-Tern Rehabilitation facility. During my clinical rotations, while in nursing school, I fell in love with the fast pace of the ED. Ambulances and people moved in and out, quick decisions had to be made in order to save lives. This was the nursing life for me and the start of a new adventure.

Talk about baptism by fire. Memorial is a large community teaching hospital, which boasts a trauma center, and a stroke center, among other services. I learned a lot, and fast, through the guidance of my amazing preceptors, mentors, and leaders. My seniors in the field demonstrated characteristics that I sought to emulate and soon my goal was nursing leadership. As a result, my continued learning led to a Bachelor Degree in Nursing (BSN) and a Master's Degree in Business (MBA).

My journey through the ED crossed several hospitals and exposed me to different specialties, especially since that's the entry point into the hospital for most patients.

Managers and mentors were always there for the staff, leading, assisting and supporting whenever and wherever required. At times when there was a shortage of staff, managers would step in and assist with direct patient care. Staff morale was high because our leaders showed that they cared.

This is what I want to achieve. However, when the time came and I advanced up the ladder, I didn't experience the same level of satisfaction, and after a short interval returned to my first love.

While working in the Emergency Department, and after many years of experience, I was introduced to the Sexual Assault Nurse Examiner job. Prior to training, my tasks included being a chaperone while the doctor performed the examination on the victim and collected the evidence, which I later packaged and maintained chain of custody, until it was handed off to law enforcement. Many doctors and nurses prefer to not care for victims because of fear that they may be called to appear in court. I have memories of doctors and nurses who were visibly upset and expressed their disdain for this process.

One particular night I was on shift when a female victim rolled into the ED with fire rescue. She was placed in a room outside of my assigned area of the department. Upon realizing what the chief complaint was, the nurse whose room she was in, marched over to the charge nurse and said, "I don't want that patient in my room."

She didn't want to care for a rape victim.

Since they were friends, without hesitation, the charge nurse moved the patient to one of my rooms. Knowing what had transpired, I felt badly for the patient and prepared to give the best care possible at a time when she needed it most. I breezed into the room where a young lady sat on the stretcher with the blanket pulled up to her chin. She was in her twenties, teary-eyed, had bruises to her face, and looked scared. When our eyes met she said, "I don't want you to be my nurse."

Dumbstruck. I stopped at the bedside and looked at her with compassion.

This scared young woman continued, "It's not you. I just don't want you to be my nurse."

Although puzzled, I said, "It's okay. I will inform the charge nurse."

When I informed her of the patient's wishes, she responded, "I will not change her nurse. You are her nurse."

Dear God. I felt badly for the patient, but the decision was out of my hands. I was the only nurse in the department that night who really wanted to care for her, and she didn't want my services. Whatever her reason for not wanting me to attend to her, I felt she was being victimized again by not having a different nurse.

I returned to her room to convey the news.

"I'm sorry," I said, "she will not change the assignment, but I'm happy to take care of you."

She looked at me for a moment, as if she could not believe I still wanted to assist her after what she had said. In the end, she was happy with my services, and thanked me multiple times throughout the process. It remained a mystery why she didn't want me to take care of her. At the time, I felt she had enough to deal with and would *not* burden her with questions that weren't relevant.

The following day I informed the Director of the incident and she agreed that the patient should have been assigned another nurse. She informed me that she would speak with the charge nurse to prevent any repeat. However, there was no follow up to ensure that the discussion had taken place.

A couple of years later, I became a trained Sexual Assault Nurse Examiner (SANE), which meant that when I, or any other trained nurse was on shift, we were automatically assigned these victims. Part of our responsibilities include independently performing the forensic examination with evidence collection unless there was a medical issue and the doctor was needed.

Nursing is my calling. Whether caring for patients in the Emergency Department or in the rape crisis center, I am passionate about the rights of victims of sexual assault, rape, domestic violence, and any other form of violence. Each role is profoundly serious to me and I pursue them with equal enthusiasm.

Over the years my training and experiences, in addition to my interactions with organizations and individuals who champion the cause of victims, have enabled me to process my own victimization and achieve some level of healing. I married my passion for nursing with victim advocacy and they are reigning harmoniously.

In my career, I've cared for numerous victims of these crimes—children and adults, both male and female. SANE is a specialty and one can choose to be certified as SANE A (Adult/Adolescent) and or SANE-P (Pediatric). My training and experience cover adult and adolescent. I have cared for the homeless and the millionaire with equal zest. Victims hold a special place in my heart due to my experiences, and those of family and friends.

As a SANE, I'm trained to first believe the victim. This is because so many victims are not believed, listened to, or validated. I recall one particular young lady burst into tears when I said, "I believe you."

She grabbed my hand and said, "Thank you for believing me."

While we talked, she relayed that at the age of five, her mother's boyfriend had raped her. However, her mother failed to believe her. As a result, she said, the abuse went unchecked for years until it was discovered by another family member.

She reported that she had been the victim of multiple family members, friends of the family, and strangers, while growing up. Here she was, still being victimized and that wasn't her first incident as an adult.

I sat on her bed and wrapped my arms around her, providing comfort for long as she needed. That is a part of what we do; the emotional support is tantamount to helping the victim begin the healing process.

My passion for victim advocacy was cemented when I relocated to Orlando, Florida, and joined the Victim Services Center of Central Florida (VSC). This organization provides coordinated, specialized services and resources to assist victims of sexual assault, violent crime, and traumatic circumstances. Their process ranges from crisis response, advocacy, therapy, and community awareness.

Victims and Survivors need encouragement and support. We hold hands and share hugs, and often may be found siting on beds or floors, as appropriate. The victim comes first. I give that one hundred percent of the time. No rush. The victim sets the pace. I sometimes wish I had been able to offer the same help to my family in their time of need, or that someone had done the same for me when I was violated. However, I don't dwell on that as I must focus on the role and person at hand. I must be present and intentional at all times.

The role of a SANE cannot be overemphasized. It's a critical part of the Sexual Assault Response Team (SART) that includes Law Enforcement, Forensic Lab, and the District Attorney, among others.

Victims of sexual violence deserve to be heard, validated, and receive the best outcome possible. The Sexual Assault Response Team is designed to provide a cohesive, multi-disciplinary body, which delivers a comprehensive response to ensure that victims are best served. This process is designed to have a positive impact from the first interaction with the victim, whether it be law enforcement, advocates or healthcare, and continues throughout the forensic and legal process, and healing/surviving.

Besides providing emotional support, medical and forensic care, the specially trained nurse also gives expert witness testimony during court proceedings, if cases advance to that stage. Most don't reach trial, either due to the perpetrator pleading out and saving the victim from reliving the trauma in open court, or lack of evidence. Sometimes, the victim may choose to abort the case. No matter where it leads, the team is there for the victim.

Most times the end of the ED visit concludes the association between the victim and SANE. However, it gives a feeling of accomplishment, when we receive feedback that the work we do make a difference and that they are appreciative.

An eighteen-year-old woman had visited the ED after being raped by two of her classmates as they drove her home from a party. I cared for her and performed the forensic examination with a specimen collection. At the time of discharge, she expressed thanks, as she left with her mother.

A few months later, while at work, a smiling young lady walked up to me and said, "You did my rape kit."

I smiled at her with recognition. "They're in jail. The DNA test came back a match, and they are in jail." She opened her arms, and we hugged and laughed in celebration.

We chatted for a while and as often happens with victims, she recounted her story of being violated.

I reminded her that it wasn't her fault and to stop self-blame. "The blame rests with the boys." I also encouraged her to continue with the therapist that she had been paired with to help her through the healing process. "You are not a victim."

"I'm a survivor," she said. "I'm a survivor."

As we talked she began to relax and her smile returned.

"Thank you," she said as we parted. "I'll never forget you."

In addition to being a trained Sexual Assault Nurse Examiner, I'm in the process of establishing my practice as a Legal Nurse Consultant (LNC). Another area in which I will be championing the cause of victims by assisting attorneys with a range of cases including medical malpractice. LNCs contribute invaluable support services—reviewing medical records in order to identify deviations from the standard of care and preparing reports among other services, which include giving expert witness testimony in court as needed.

FIRST MARRIAGE

Roy and I met at the Jamaica Public Service Company, in May Pen, where I worked as a secretary, and he a lineman. He was wonderful and funny, and I enjoyed his company. Roy was graced with a good physique and a bright smile. He later migrated to the United States and we kept in touch. Over time, the tone of our friendship changed and became a romantic one. A few years later, he returned to Jamaica and our relationship blossomed as we continued to spend more time together, and got to know each other better. We continued dating and got married in 1986. He continued to live in the United States and through the immigration proceedings, I joined him there in 1989.

Little did I know I had married a womanizer. When I moved to the United States, there were no friends or family close by. One of my friends in Jamaica had given me contact information for her aunt, who I reached out to soon after I arrived, and we developed a friendship.

A short time after living with my then husband, I was reorganizing the master bedroom closet when a stack of paper fell from a shelf. As I gathered the envelopes, some of the contents fell out. I discovered love letters women had written to my husband while I was in Jamaica. Some were written during our marriage. Of note, one of the letters was from the woman who showed up at my job in Jamaica and handed me the airline ticket for my trip to the United States. I guess she happened to be in America visiting him at the time. As I sat on the floor, in the closet and bawled, I felt like a fool. How could he do this to me? How could someone who appeared to be so nice and great husband material turn out to be such a fraud?

"What are these?" I asked when he returned from work, as I held out the bundle towards him.

He took the letters. "Why are you searching my place?"

"Is that all you have to say to me?"

He shook his head and walked away.

Soon discovered that his cheating ways weren't behind him. I was living with a serial Casanova.

After I made the discovery, my curiosity was piqued, so I observed his daily habits. Sadly, I must admit, a few times I jumped in my car and followed him to see where he was and later confronted him. I would locate his car in the parking lot of some woman's apartment. When I returned home, I would dial their number and yell, "Stay away from my husband," and hang up. No explanation was needed, since they knew who I was. These were women who knew me, and us as a couple. He always returned home angry, but I would repeat the action. Some nights he didn't return home. Many sleepless nights, I wondered where he was and with whom.

His infidelity continued until we divorced in 1997.

My first marriage was difficult and unhappy. We separated twice, prior to finally divorcing. The first time we split, he was contrite and begged for forgiveness. He even went to our pastor and asked for his intervention in brokering a reconciliation. Friends of mine encouraged me not to return to the marriage, and others advised that I give it another try. These were friends we knew from Jamaica, church, and work. Friends who had our best interest in mind. On several occasions he showed up at my job with beautiful floral arrangements.

I was *not* impressed.

Where were those bouquets during our years of marriage? Why now? He earned sympathy and praise from some of my coworkers. As a result, they often wondered why I remained unmoved by such romantic gestures.

As time progressed, and he was persistent, I prayed about it, talked to my pastor, and other friends. Eventually, I relented, returned home, and we renewed our vows at a ceremony in church. However, the happiness was short-lived. Within a month he was back to philandering, even cheated with women who were living on the same condominium complex where we resided. Phone calls came in the middle of the night and early in the morning, before we got out of bed. He often stayed out overnight.

I was silent most of the time because I'm not good at confrontation. Sometimes, for days we exchanged no words. The silence was deafening.

I found other women's utility bills that he paid, hidden in his vehicle, while there were times when we needed the money. All these women that I became aware of were from Jamaica. I don't mean to imply this behavior is unique to Jamaican women. At the time, I thought a Jamaican woman would be more thoughtful of another of the same culture. A sort of sisterhood, I guess. However, to be honest, sometimes I thought of it as payback for the times when both my mother and I dated married men. I knew then how those wives had felt. Sad and humiliated.

Finally, when I decided to put my mental health first, I informed him that the marriage was over and it was time for a divorce. His response, is lost from my memory, and it wouldn't have mattered. The divorce papers were filed and with the intervention of mutual friends the process was quickly settled. I never discussed my marriage with my family in Jamaica. However, when my it ended, my mother said, "I knew you weren't happy."

A mother always knows.

During our marriage, there were occasions when I didn't want to go home. My home wasn't my happy place and it should have been. I was married, lonely, and sad, with suicidal thoughts. Thank God, I never developed a plan, and I'm here today to hopefully help someone by telling my story.

Many nights, I got into my car and drove for miles—destination unknown. Several times, I entertained the thought that I didn't want to be around anymore and ended up in totally foreign locations. If it weren't for GPS, I don't know what may have happened to me. I thank the good Lord for keeping me safe and sane.

Psalm 121:8 *"The Lord shall preserve your going out and your coming in..."*

During one of my visits to Jamaica, I was chatting with a group of friends who happened to be sisters. The topic of suicide came up because of a story in the news. The oldest said, "I would never commit suicide. There is nothing that might happen to me that I couldn't discuss with one of my sisters."

Her sisters, which included me, looked at her and nodded. I never mentioned when I was depressed and had thoughts of suicide. Thank God that was no longer my reality.

After the divorce, Roy and I maintained contact and when I bought my house, he installed my new lighting fixtures because he is an electrician by trade.

One day, after he replaced a light, I was surprised when he turned to me and said, "Marie, will you marry me."

Where did that come from? I had never said or given him any indication there would be any rekindling of our relationship. He never stated or indicated any such desire in any of our interactions before now. Otherwise, he wouldn't have been welcomed in my home.

There was no need for a response.

Veda Angel didn't raise a fool. That bridge was crossed and burned.

Once the divorce was finalized, I received calls and texts from friends and acquaintances, young and old. They congratulated me on my strength and bravery, and expressed sorrow that they didn't have the courage to do the same. However, I didn't feel strong or brave—I felt sick, tired, and ashamed, of what I endured all those years.

Many women and men remain in unhappy and unhealthy marriages, for various reasons. One eighty-five-year-old woman said, "I wish I had been brave to leave mine. I just found out that he has a fifteen-year-old son in Jamaica." She continued, "He has cheated on me many times over the years, even with a neighbor. But what am I supposed to do? I am a Christian and I don't believe in divorce."

I replied, "It's not the will of God that I should be sick, tired, ashamed, and unhappy in any relationship or marriage. Not the God I serve."

She had no response. I suggested she pray and have a talk with her pastor.

Dear Lord, have mercy.

Life wasn't all sadness during my marriage. When I arrived in the States, I was Marie McKenzie, Secretary, and when the marriage ended, Licensed Practical Nurse, in college to become a Registered Nurse. No matter where you are in life, if you seek God, He will lead you to your purpose.

MY HALLELUJAH! MY GEORGE

One Friday in February 2002, my five-year-old white Mazda 626 gave out while I was at work. Two days later I asked my friend, Tony, to accompany me on a car shopping expedition. I wasn't going to wait to have my Mazda examined at a repair shop. Since it was over five years old, I determined that it was near death, and expected more problems afterwards.

Tony and I pulled into Coconut Creek Mitsubishi. Three men walked briskly toward us, two were White and one Black. The Black man reminded me of a linebacker in the NFL. He left the others behind and approached me first, introduced himself, and enquired about my needs as he led me to the showroom and his office.

After ascertaining my specific needs, we went to the car lot to see what was available. I settled on a dark-colored Mitsubishi Galant, and was satisfied with my purchase when I left, and thought that was the end of that.

A few days later, I had the Mazda towed to the mechanic and was pleasantly surprised when informed that all it needed was a forty-dollar hose. By then, I had the new car and happily called my pastor and donated the old one to the church. It became a blessing to someone else.

Come Monday evening, it was time for my night shift. I pulled onto I-95 and headed South, but didn't get far because one of the tires blew out. I called a road ranger, got patched up, and continued on my way to work.

Tuesday morning, I returned to the dealership to report what had happened, and have my tire changed. They arranged for a chauffeur to drive me home while my car was being fixed. From there I called my salesperson, George, and told him about my dilemma.

He replied, "Tell them to call me when you get here."

When I returned to pick up my car, I asked one of the employees at the dealership to call George.

He arrived with a big grin on his face, then ensured that the car was ready and acceptable. To my surprise, he hugged me while saying goodbye. As I was about to leave, he said, "Can you introduce me to one of your nice, single nurse friends?"

While chatting with George the first time I was there, I told him I was a nurse.

I smiled and responded, "I'm nice and I'm single."

We both laughed and parted ways. I headed home, sure that was our final meeting.

Two days later, my phone rang and it was George enquiring about the state of my car. I assured him that everything was all right and it was running like a well-oiled clock. He said goodbye, then hung up.

Friday of that same week, he called again. "Are you off from work on Saturday?"

I hesitated to answer, then replied, "Yes, I will be off."

George then asked, "May I invite you to dinner?"

He is going all out.

"Yes," I replied.

I thought he must have felt badly about what happened to my car and was extending customer service at an extremely elevated level—which is why I agreed to dinner the following evening. If I ever had the slightest feeling that he was making a pass at me, I would have never agreed. But he was charming and didn't appear to have an ulterior motive.

He took me to the Olive Gardens in Plantation. This was one of the best nights of my life. We clicked immediately, and I didn't want the night to end.

After dinner, he took me for a walk along the beach and showed me a house he admired. I later learned that scoping out properties was one of his favorite hobbies. We have since visited hundreds of open houses, even when we weren't shopping for a home. We became inseparable, and in less than two months after our initial meeting, we planned our wedding.

George generates warmth, and all my friends love him as soon as they meet. While we were dating, my friend Monique, visited and met him. "Oh, my God," she whispered, "Marie, are you taking your vitamins?"

We giggled like teenagers. Yes! Five feet eleven inches, two hundred and fifteen pounds, shoulders and biceps like he had been pumping iron for years, and a six pack. Yeah, baby, he's my eye candy.

After dealing with a philandering husband and divorce, I decided to remain free and single. However, that changed with George. I was anxiously awaiting marriage. My happiness was palpable.

The day before our wedding, some of my female friends and I gathered to finalize plans and relax for the upcoming event. My uncle, Clovis, mentioned that in England the ladies held a hen party for the bride.

"What is a hen party?" I asked.

He explained, and we realized it was similar to a bachelorette party.

We hadn't planned to have one, but at that time I banged my hand on the table and said, "I want a hen party."

My "hens" sprang into action and shortly thereafter, we were seated in one of the local restaurants having fun.

Donna was my chief wedding planner, who was businesslike, professional, and full of grace. She gave out of town visitors local hotel information, and other instructions, to ensure that they were all comfortable. My crew was extraordinary, and even confiscated my cellphone the day prior to the wedding, and kept me out of the finishing touches. They banned me to the extent that when I arrived at the reception, I realized the flowers weren't what we had ordered. I later learned of the mishaps and how we almost lost the wedding cake during transport. The stories were hilarious.

On November 30, 2002, we said our "I dos" in the presence of friends and family.

My second wedding was magical and perfect. I had the man of my dreams and the special people I wanted were present. Our friends and family travelled from Jamaica and different states in the USA, and England.

Nineteen years plus, and he still makes my heart sing.

With my George, I learned what it is to be loved and protected by a man. I now know what a loving, healthy marriage is. I also know what it feels like to be cherished and adored. Almost daily since we became a couple, he kisses me and says, "I love you."

As a nurse, I work the night shift and pride myself for being on time. One evening as I prepared to leave home, George yanked the back of my scrub top and remarked, "You have a butt in that thing."

I laughed and turned to face him. Well, work could wait this one time.

With George, I experienced what I believe the heroines in my favorite Mills & Boon and Harlequin romance novels felt. Raw heat, toe-curling, heart-pounding passion. I wish this for every woman, even once.

Since we met, I have received numerous bouquets of beautiful flowers, not just on special occasions, and certainly not as an apology. I have preserved every flower from those arrangements.

Pity my mother didn't live to meet him. I would have loved for her to know that I'm happy.

Prior to meeting George, coworkers called me stoic, and family members labeled me as being too strict. I thought I was professional and businesslike. My brother O'Keile, told him, "Thank you for saving my sister."

He relayed that now I'm more relaxed and didn't take everything so seriously.

George chuckled, then said, "I got her, O'Keile."

Yes, that *is* true. I had to evaluate my life and make changes. I learned to stop being impulsive and avoid activities that weren't compatible with the life that I wanted. The life of a Christian woman. Someone who wanted to put God first and follow his teachings. After a while, I realized that in so doing I had gone to extremes. As a result, I was overly firm with the children in the family. So much so, they were in a constant state of alertness whenever I was around them. Looking back, I accept that I had been overly zealous.

Now, I'm joyful and relaxed and family members, young and old, enjoy my company. Being in this loving marriage has resulted in significant improvement in my overall wellbeing, especially my mental health. When you are feeling good about yourself, it shows, and causes others to want to spend time with you.

My nephew's wife, Sudene, sent me this text during the time I was writing this book. "Good evening, aunty. You came to my thoughts today and I was reminded of the awesome person you are. I know we didn't spend a long time around each other, but what I have seen and experienced around you is enough for me to say that you are someone to be admired. Keep on being the genuine and principled woman you are. God bless you."

This warmed my heart and stirred tears. Prior to finding joy and happiness with George, I don't believe she would have felt the same about me.

We may never have met, because my nephew might not have been willing to expose his family to me because of my temperament back when they were growing up. For reasons unknown, most times I was angry, yelled at them for simple things and acted like I expected them to be perfect at all times.

Most times I wasn't pleasant company with relatives. Being home brought out the sadness in me. I remembered too much of what had happened there.

CHURCH

We grew up in the church. As far back as I can remember, I went because it was mandatory. Later, I continued because I enjoyed the singing, clapping, and the cymbals. During my young adulthood, I attended Sunday service in the afternoons because it continued for hours. What is it about Jamaican churches with the l-o-n-g Sunday services?

Conventions and other organized programs were special for me. Through these events, I developed an extraordinary memory and practiced my public speaking. I didn't recognize these advantages at that time. My aunt, Sister Herma, provided special poems for me to recite at these events, most of which were taken from the bible and often involved whole chapters. One of my fondest recollections was when I belted out Isaiah 53, from beginning to end, at one convention, where I received a standing ovation.

Since church was special to me, when I relocated to the United States, with the help of my friend's aunt, I quickly identified a spiritual home and started attending.

Although I relished the fellowship and sermons of the US church, I was puzzled by the approach to offering. The activities were sometimes treated as *fundraisers*. Don't get me wrong, I do believe it is important to contribute to the church. I grew up tithing ten percent of my earnings, no matter how minimal. However, that changed.

One Sunday, the moderator said, "If I should multiply by ten what some of you give, and give it back, you wouldn't be able to live off it."

Really? How dare she? Due to my situation at that time, it was personal for me and I became angry. As a part-time clerical worker, my gross salary was one hundred and twenty-seven dollars and a few cents each week. Yet, I religiously tithed ten percent and rounded up to an even amount. Until *that* day, I had been committed to tithing.

Since then, I have refocused my giving, although I still contribute money to the church. I have dedicated my time and finances to serving the needy, wherever I find them. Whether it be charitable organizations, friends, family, strangers, or coworkers in need. Sometimes it's a patient, or their family.

Scriptures state, "...to whom much is given, much is required..." (Luke 12:48).

Although I grew up in the church and had a solid Christian foundation, I strayed and travelled many wrong roads along the way.

Thanks to my aunt Herma, who not only preached, but lived the talk, I gradually returned to my faith, especially after getting to know the Briscoes. The family demonstrated a complete surrender to God through their daily living. Unshakable faith, which I strongly embraced. I knew that God would bring me through the fire and over the mountain.

The Lord is my Shephard.

REFLECTIONS

As a young adult, my desire was to get married and have two sons. I always believed that we needed more good men in the world and that I would be a great mother and mentor. However, with both of my marriages, I inherited four lovely daughters, two from each. God does have a sense of humor.

I have made a few turns on my journey that I'm not proud of, and each held experiences that I have learned from and grown through.

One such turn was dating a man who wasn't single. At the time, I didn't think how wrong that was, and that I was hurting another woman and also myself and my reputation. After all, I was continuing the cycle by following in the footsteps of my mother and grandmother. It was one of the most egregious acts I have ever committed. We are all responsible for our own actions. I knew better and should have done otherwise.

Thank God for His grace, my journey is different now.

Have you ever received a message from God? *I have*. During a period of severe despair and depression, I chastised myself, "You are just like your mother."

One Saturday night, I was alone in my home, a sense of overwhelming hopelessness came over me and I cried out to God. "God, help me, I do *not* want to be like my mother. Here I'm repeating the things I disapproved of about her lifestyle. Help me, Lord. Forgive me, Lord, and change my heart."

Another sleepless night!

Sunday was church as usual, a time of renewal for me, and I went with great expectation. We had a guest pastor that Sunday. He was young, charismatic, and appeared to be a real servant of God. During the sermon, he looked at me and said, "You are not like your mother. *You* are not your mother." I don't remember anything else he said that day. Not the message or the scriptures.

I lost it. The tears flowed freely. *Prayer answered. Thank you Jesus.*

Amazing grace! Amazing grace! Thank God for grace.

My life experiences and that of my family have led to insomnia, depression, suicidal thoughts, abnormal eating, and lack of self-esteem.

I thank the Lord that He has placed people and resources in my life that have helped me to overcome. As a result, I now use the lessons learned to help others.

Use me Lord, for Your glory.

SURVIVOR: THE HEALING JOURNEY

Do not cry for the little girl who was.
Rejoice with, and for, the woman who is.
Author: Marie McKenzie

After my memoir, *Things That Keep Me Up at Night*, was written, I felt that the recesses of my mind were searched and cleansed and that my nightmares were over. The thought was, the bad dreams were buried, and sleep would finally take hold of me. Finally, all was put to rest and the title should be changed to, Things that Kept me up at Nights. However, as I re-read and edited my story, I came to realize, the journey will be lifelong. Although less troubling, like an addict, my recovery is a continuing process.

BREAKING THE SILENCE

The things that keep me up at night are fading because I refuse to let them continue to hold me hostage. Being a Sexual Assault Nurse Examiner and interacting with other advocates and organizations has brought home the benefits of breaking the silence, for me as well as others. I have come to realize the importance of using my voice. Opening my mouth has loosened the fear that had a vise grip around my heart all these years.

Speaking out and writing have brought me a sense of freedom I have never known. I'm shouting – *no more silence or shame!*

I'm a girl from Jamaica who has walked through the fire, and although scathed, got through to the other side with my head held high. I'm a survivor and I'm thriving. To God be the glory. I would not have made it without the Lord's help. Every step of the way, He has placed people and resources in my corner to guide, encourage, and support me. My journey wasn't rosy, nor did I act appropriately at all times. I'm not an angel as you can tell from my story. All of my missteps came with consequences.

Throughout my journey, I have realized that sharing my history and pain with others has allowed me to receive comfort and healing.

This book is not about embarrassing anyone, but mostly for me. In sharing my story, I hope to help others see how they may do things differently to positively impact the ones who are, or may be, looking to them for love and guidance. My intention is to show someone that you can rise, survive, and thrive despite adversity.

Parents, educate your children about sexual violence and what to do if they experience it, and keep an open line of communication. Please, refrain from telling them to shut up when they show curiosity about life matters. In Jamaica, as a child I was often told, "Shut up! Children must be seen and not heard." Well, I kept quiet! But my silence didn't serve me well.

Children have a voice and need to be heard. It is my hope that this book will encourage others to break the silence, especially the young ones.

Through the grace of God, I emerged from that life, not unscathed, but now happy and prosperous. I stepped out of the shadows of a sad, lonely child into the life of a strong, healthy, happy, and vibrant woman. Now, I realize that at every step of the way, the Lord placed people in my life to help, encourage, and inspire me on my journey. I consider myself blessed and highly favored. My experiences have had helped to shape the woman I am today, so I don't live with regret. My story is not about a happy, perfect, or sad life. It is my tale of resilience and triumph that I share to encourage and inspire someone who may have gone through, or is encountering similar circumstances. You can rise above your beginnings. You can survive and thrive!

LET'S HELP TO END THIS MADNESS

Sexual violence is not okay.

Domestic violence is not okay.

Any form of violence/abuse is not okay.

Sexual violence affects men, women and children of any age, nationality, sexual orientation and economic status.

Evil does not discriminate.

Victims often end up with devastating lifelong side effects. Perpetrators include parents, spouses, family members, acquaintances, friends or strangers from all walks of life. They may be in the pulpit or pew in your church, on the bench in court, or standing at a chalk board in our school, coaching your children's sports team, just to list a few.

Evil is everywhere.

Sexual violence occurs when someone engages in sexual acts when consent is not obtained or freely given. The absence of consent may be due to, but not limited to, being incapacitated by drugs or alcohol, fear, disability, and age.

Sexual violence is not limited to rape, but also includes touching or other sexual contact, harassment, exposing private parts, or nakedness, masturbating in open areas, and voyeurism.

The statistics are staggering.

According to The National Intimate Partner and Sexual Violence Survey of 2010:

In Florida, one in six women have been raped at some point in their lives. In addition, over three million have experienced sexual violence other than rape. Approximately eighty percent of female rape victims experienced their first rape before the age of twenty-five, with forty two percent before their eighteenth birthday.

Additionally, more than one million men have been victims of sexual violence other than rape. About twenty-eight percent of males who experienced rape, had their first incident at ten years of age or younger.

This data only reflects reported rapes and sexual assaults. It must be noted that most victims don't make a report. Rape is the most underreported crime against children and adults.

Don't equate rape with sex. Rape is about exerting power and control over a victim.

If you, or someone you know, have been a victim of rape, sexual, or domestic violence please seek help. There are numerous community and national resources available, even if you don't want to involve law enforcement. If you are in a situation where your life is at risk call 911.

The effects that sexual violence has on some victims can be life threatening or last a lifetime. Some suffer from Post-Traumatic Stress Disorder (PTSD), drug and alcohol abuse, suicidal and homicidal ideations, suicide or attempted suicide, dysfunctional relationships with family, spouse and other partners. Some are unable to maintain employment and suffer from long-term mental illness like anxiety and depression.

Some victims also unconsciously act out their victimization. One informed me, she was first abused by her twenty-year-old cousin, when she was eight years old. "He gave me money and nice clothes and often promised me gifts." She continued, "When I was older I would freely have sex with boys at school, or men, if I received or was promised money or gifts. I never made the connection until I sought therapy."

She told me she had never mentioned the abuse to anyone except her therapist.

Let's end the silence.

Whether you are a perpetrator or a victim, please get help, it's never too late.

MY PRAYER

I prayed To God

For Him to open my eyes

So that I may see the path He has laid out for me.

I prayed to God

For Him to open my ears that I may hear the words He is saying to me.

I prayed to God

For Him to open my heart to receive the blessings He has for me.

I prayed to God

For Him to open my mouth that I may sing His praises daily.

I prayed to God

For Him to grant me the wisdom to acknowledge all He has done, is doing, and will be doing for me.

I prayed to God. I prayed. I prayed. I prayed to God.

My desire is to use all my senses to live for Him every day and that His purpose will be fulfilled in me.

I pray to God. I pray. I pray.

Author: Marie McKenzie

MARIE L. MCKENZIE

Marie McKenzie is an accomplished and experienced Registered Nurse, educator, community volunteer, victims' advocate, and trained Sexual Assault Nurse Examiner. Born in Jamaica, Marie migrated to the United States of America in 1989 and has over twenty-three years of experience in her chosen field.

When she is not on the job, Marie volunteers and advocates for survivors of sexual violence, domestic violence and the homeless. She has volunteered for food banks, crisis pregnancy centers, and homeless organizations. Marie is a past board member of the Inner Truth Project, which strives to change the conversation surrounding sexual violence and help survivors find their voices.

https://marielmckenzie.com
https://Sociatap.com/MarieL

Alicia Mitchell, is and was, the only woman Dallas Avery ever loved. He strives to manage her fears surrounding their age difference and is determined to make her his forever. A Durabia trip will either seal the deal or will force them to part ways.

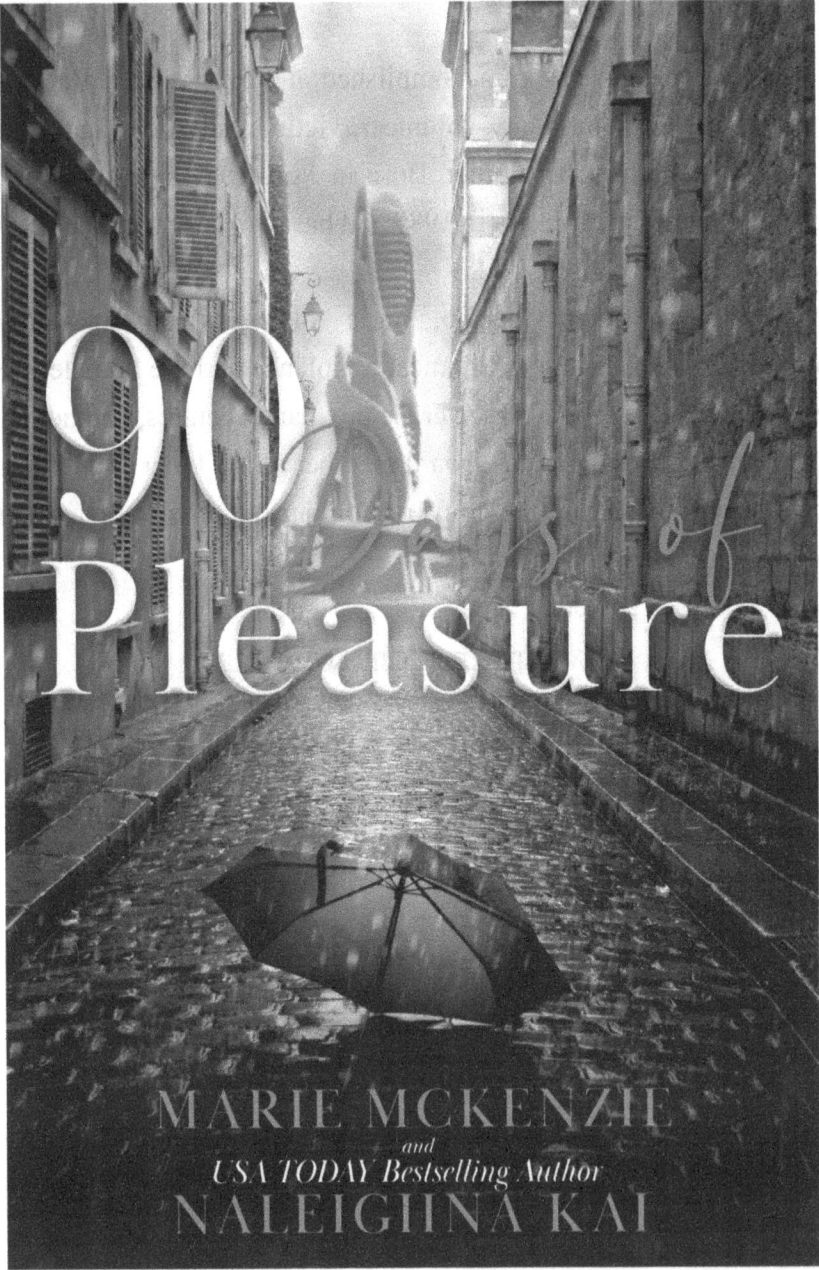

90 Days of
Pleasure

MARIE MCKENZIE
and
USA TODAY Bestselling Author
NALEIGHNA KAI

FROM THE PROJECTS TO A PH.D.
A VIEW FROM THE OTHER SIDE OF AMERICA
DR. VANESSA HOWARD

Things that keep me up at Night
Marie McKenzie

Single Again?
HOW TO LIVE SATISFIED UNTIL ...
Erica B. Davis

Growing Up
Joplin
KADESHA POWELL

An inspirational standalone book series that will warm your heart and touch your soul...

TRANSITION
NALEIGHNA KAI

VISION
J.L. CAMPBELL

JOURNEY
LISA DODSON

GROWTH
JANICE M. ALLEN

CHOICES
PAT G. OKItE-WALKER

PERSISTENCE
U.M. HIRAM

PURPOSE
TERRENCE JENKINS

PATIENCE
TERRI-ANN JOHNSON

TRANSFORMATION
NALEIGHNA KAI

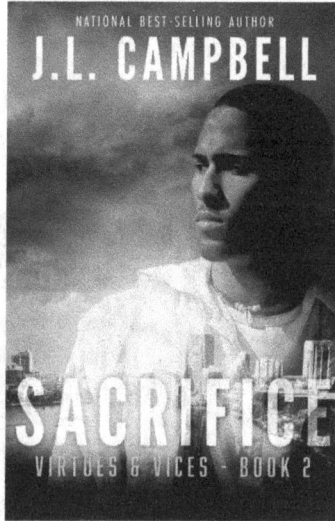

Guilt is a bitter enemy when you sacrifice one precious gift for another. Dane's two-year-old daughter is the center of his world, and doubly precious because of her health challenges. When he discovers a son from a previous relationship, his world implodes. No matter what path he takes, everything he holds dear is at stake, and life will never look the way it did before tragedy knocked at his door.

Between family drama and her weight issues, Sophie is struggling to cope. Then, her greatest fear becomes reality when she loses her daughter. Making it from one day to the next seems impossible, her trust in Dane is at an all-time low, and so is her morale. All she has is her faith, an unlikely stopgap, and the hope that everything will fall together rather than apart.

****** Sacrifice is inspirational fiction that features a couple grappling with profound loss that can end a marriage. It brings a message of faith during a time when so many are dealing with unexpected losses of one kind or another.

books by Naleighna Kai

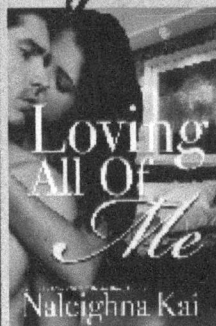

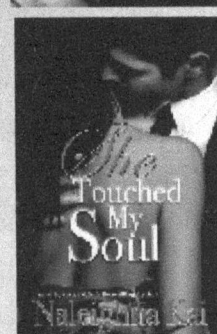

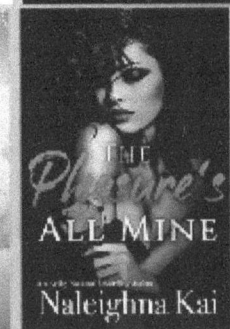

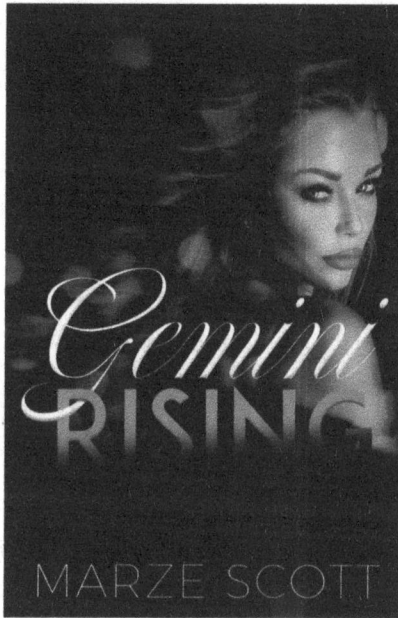

Her mother gave her to a man that broke her body and soul. Now, Gemini will be Ruthless in reclaiming her freedom.

Aisha couldn't have known how much her existence would change the summer before her tenth birthday. Her family, and life as she knew it, was turned upside down after a tragic accident that left her an only child and her mother widowed. A family secret and an arrangement sent her two hundred fifty miles from home only to be given into the hands of her treacherous new guardian, Angel. A new identity and routine were given in exchange for her freedom—Gemini was born.

Twelve years later and a turn of events uncovers her secret and now she has to figure out how to reclaim her freedom without getting herself killed.

www.marzescott.com
www.facebook.com/marzescott
www.instagram.com/marzefab

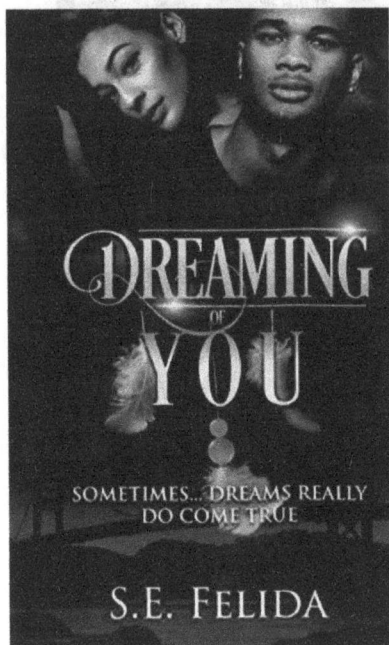

She dreamed of him before ever meeting him...

He found her when she needed him the most...

When Leona sees the guy she dreamed about, she decides not to approach him out of the bizarreness of the whole situation. Fate, on the other hand, seems to differ, and redirects him, Nathaniel, toward Leona again in her time of need.

Nathaniel, a police officer who's been on the hunt to find his little brother's killer for over a year now, turns out to be a dream guy in real life too. Although things are going great between him and Leona, someone is out to ruin his life and crush his dream to avenge Isaac's death.

Will Leona and Nathaniel's love conquer all the obstacles that are about to come their way?

Find out in *Dreaming of You...*

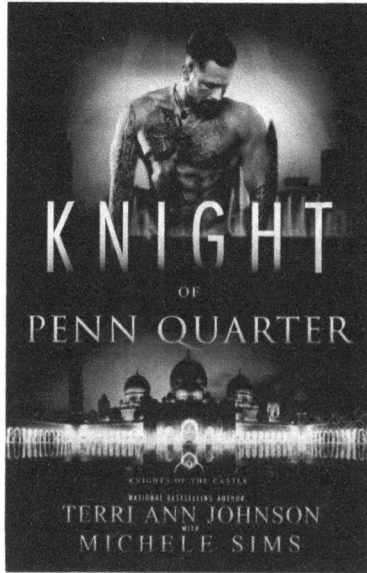

KNIGHT
OF
PENN QUARTER

KNIGHTS OF THE CASTLE
NATIONAL BESTSELLING AUTHOR
TERRI ANN JOHNSON
WITH
MICHELE SIMS

Following an undercover FBI sting operation that didn't go as planned, Agent Mateo Lopez is ready to put the government agency in his rearview mirror.

A confirmed workaholic, his career soared at the cost of his love life which had crashed and burned until mutual friends arranged a date with beautiful, sharp-witted, Rachel Jordan, a rising star at a children's social services agency.

Unlucky in love, Rachel has sworn off romantic relationships, but Mateo finds himself falling for her in more ways than one. When trouble brews in one of Ra-chel's cases, he does everything in his power to keep her safe – even if it means resort-ing to extreme measures.

Will the choices they make bring them closer together or cost them their lives?

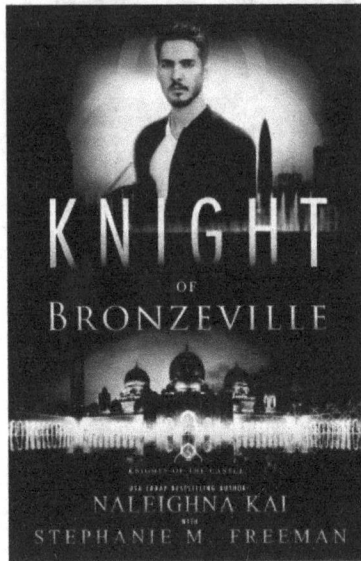

KNIGHT
OF
BRONZEVILLE

KNIGHTS OF THE CASTLE
USA TODAY BESTSELLING AUTHOR
NALEIGHNA KAI
WITH
STEPHANIE M. FREEMAN

Chaz Maharaj thought he could maintain the lie of a perfect marriage for his adoring fans … until he met Amanda. The connection between them should have ended with that unconditional "hall pass" which led to one night of unbridled passion. But once would never satisfy his hunger for a woman who could never be his. When Amanda walked out of his life, it was supposed to be forever. Neither of them could have anticipated fate's plan.

Chaz wants to explore his feelings for Amanda, but Susan has other ideas. Prepared to fight for his budding romance and navigate a plot that's been laid to crush them, an unexpected twist threatens his love and her life. When Amanda's past comes back to haunt them, Chaz enlists the Kings of the Castle to save his newfound love in a daring escape.